D0581303

The Forward Poetry Prizes are supported by Forward, one of the UK's leading multi-channel content agencies. Forward creates beautifully crafted, highly targeted customer communications for clients such as Patek Philippe, Ford, Tesco, Standard Life, Porto Montenegro, Regus and Barclays. Forward's bespoke magazines, websites, ezines and emails are produced in 38 languages and reach customers in 172 countries. For more information, please visit www.theforwardgroup.com

The Forward book of poetry
2013

London

First published in Great Britain by
Forward Ltd · 84–86 Regent Street · London W1B 5RR
in association with
Faber and Faber · Bloomsbury House · 74–77 Great Russell Street ·
London WC1B 3DA

ISBN 978 0 571 29901 0 (paperback)

Compilation copyright © Forward Ltd 2012
Foreword copyright © Leonie Rushforth

Printed and bound by CPI Group (UK) Ltd, Croydon, CR0 4YY

Cover: Alamy, Comstock, Dreamstime, Getty, Istock

MIX
Paper from
responsible sources
FSC
www.fsc.org
FSC® C016486

A CIP catalogue reference for this book
is available at the British Library.

To Matilda Kent. In memoriam

Contents

Highly Commended Poems 2012

Foreword

AT THE TIME OF WRITING we are half way through a very wet July and
the process of the Forward judging; the shortlists will be published later
this week and we are about to set off on what, in comparison with the
first stage of things, will be a luxurious two months to get to know better
the ten shortlisted collections and the five single poems. Meanwhile this
anthology will be printed and we hope when it appears it will give not
only a representative sample of each of the shortlisted titles in company
with the contenders for best single poem, but also a broader view of the
reading we have done, the choices we made at different stages and by
implication the discussions that went on. It gives us the opportunity to
acknowledge some of the many hundreds of poems we read and loved,
and have had to let go of as we winnowed our way to a smaller and
smaller number of titles.

In yesterday's *Guardian* Paul Bailey wrote about his dislike of the
hoopla surrounding the big annual novel prizes and of the 'horsetrading
and bargaining that was a feature of the judging process' he was at one
time involved in. It may be because there is less at stake financially for
other parties in the longer run that the process for a poetry prize is
less combative and ritualistic; whatever the reason, I can attest that the
discussions we have had have been characterised by a willingness to put
our personal criteria to the test and a desire that the shortlists should
represent both individual conviction and agreement on which collections
we, collectively, most wanted to go on reading and re-reading. And
perhaps this is a moment to thank the publishers who submitted titles
to this year's Forward prizes for continuing to take the risks they do for
the love of the poetry they find. One hundred and seventy collections
were sent in, and the five of us – Emma Hogan, Ian McMillan, Alice
Oswald, Megan Walsh and myself – each read all of them.

We arrived at the shortlisting meeting after weeks of solitary decision
making and were very ready to argue fiercely for the best we had found.
What then happened was both passionate advocacy and a reassessment
of our judgements in the light of others that differed from them. The
enjoyable outcome was highly engaged and flexible talk about poetry
from the privileged vantage point of having read what the publishers
considered the most impressive collections on their lists this year, and

in an arena delightfully free of axes being ground. It seems worth describing some of this because poetry prizes are rarely credited as drivers of the kind of talk that poets and readers of poetry alike need if they are to stand on any sort of interesting common ground. A contribution to this serious conversation is one of the spin-offs from competitions and prizes every year, beginning in the judges' meetings but more importantly spreading to wider circles where an interest is taken in how poetry is weighed by its readers.

Deciding whether and why one poem is better than another, or one collection more successful than another, is perhaps a common enough event for any committed reader of poetry pursuing and developing their individual taste, but public debate about the criteria by which such judgements are made is less available to us as an experience. It is something (though only something) like the difference between expressing opinions on questions of crime and punishment, and finding oneself called up for jury service where those opinions are brought up against very divergent positions, are subjected to sometimes uncomfortable scrutiny, and where one is very immediately responsible for the kind of discussion that evolves. Like any jury's, the judges' discussions are not made public and this relative privacy guarantees the debate does not have to take on aspects of a performance; but the five of us were for the duration of our talk, and after weeks of isolation, each other's very welcome public. The Forward anthology represents annually the agreed outcome of such a debate and we hope it might play a part in feeding others with a less pressing task and no deadline, and so perhaps more able to develop further the terms in which an exacting reading public might express what it admires in and what it wants from its poets.

I am very grateful to my fellow judges for their commitment to and generous participation in this process, and look forward to our meeting again in October to make our final decisions. I know they would join me in thanking all the poets whose work we have had the privilege to read. We hope you, the readers of this anthology, will enjoy reading and interrogating our selection.

Leonie Rushforth, *July 2012*

Preface

ONE OF THE TOUGHEST THINGS about introducing an anthology like
The Forward book of poetry is that, having read such a wide selection
of the year's best collections and individual poems, one feels almost
duty-bound to try and sum up the year in some way – or, if you like,
to search for signs of that elusive animal, the Zeitgeist. Thankfully
the landscape of contemporary poetry is too richly varied to accept
easy categorisation, yet it remains an enjoyable game (and game
is all it is) to see how particular subjects, titles and even locations
emerge from the mix.

This year, to take a few random examples, we have a barn, birds,
bees, marigolds, mermaids, mothers, McDonald's (twice); poems
set in 1944, 1950 (twice), 1960 and 1966, in France, Wisconsin and
(twice) Peckham. I'm not sure what this tells us about contemporary
English-language poetry, but I do think it tells us one thing: that
poetry remains a wonderfully diverse and vital way of responding
to the world, whether it's the world of things and places or the world
inside our head.

Of course there would be no *Forward book of poetry* without the
panel of judges who, every year, have the daunting (but by all accounts
enjoyable) task of sifting through hundreds of poems to produce
this shortlist. So my thanks go to this year's judges: Emma Hogan,
Ian McMillan, Alice Oswald and Megan Walsh, together with their
dedicated chair, Leonie Rushforth. I must also thank the team at
Colman Getty who, each year, do so much to help spread the word:
Dotti Irving, Liz Sich, Truda Spruyt, Chris Baker and Laura Norton.

And last but not least, my thanks to everyone at Forward, without
whom there would be no Forward Prize, and particularly to our
own winning team of Will Scott, Casey Jones, Cassia Geller and
Christopher Stocks. I hope you enjoy reading this year's anthology
as much as I have.

William Sieghart

Shortlisted Poems
The Forward Prize for Best Collection

Beverley Bie Brahic

White Sheets

Airstrike hits wedding party – breaking news

The empty laundry basket
fills with molecules of light.
She stands beside it, arms falling
into the aftermath of the task.
Gesture is a proto-language
researchers say: the same circuits
light the brain when a chimp
signals help me please (hand
outstretched, palm up) as when
human beings process speech.
In the cave the hunter figure
mirrors his spear's trajectory
towards the deer it will never,
of course, attain. The woman
sees nothing untoward. Her body
bars the spattered something
in the middle distance, though all
of this is right up close: the shed
they'll use to dress the meat, the plane
geometry of white sheets
on a line. The world is beautiful,
she thinks, or feels, as deer
sense something coming
and move out of range. Beautiful,
the woman thinks, and lifts
the laundry basket to her arms –
beautiful, and orderly.

ON THE PATHETIC FALLACY

A bird bangs your window – no tender lamb,
no Corinna, just you
with your feet up, Reader, reading, and a sheet of glass
between you, the tree
and the carport's tarpaper roof. It's a real bird
(now you hunt
for its name): it's a *genus* something
species something, it's not some despair of your own
masquerading as a bird.
Bigger than a sparrow, with a black hood. Beak dipped
in egg yolk.
Body two-tone, like a fifties Chevrolet – here it is, Reader,
you found it! *Junco*
hyemalis (16 cm [6 ¼ in] long).

Why does this '*Junco hyemalis*'
(if that's its name) keep
thrashing at the pane? Another bird, a bird
it doesn't know
is a double of itself? Reflection,
rival, or a mate,
another Junco on a winter branch of the birch
tree at your window,
near the carport roof? Wave your arms,
Reader, shout! No good. You're trapped
behind glass, in a box, in far away
repeat repeat repeat repeat repeat repeat repeat repeat repeat re-
why should it ever stop?

Jorie Graham

CAGNES SUR MER 1950

I am the only one who ever lived who remembers
my mother's voice in the particular shadow
cast by the skyfilled Roman archway
which darkens the stones on the down-sloping street
up which she has now come again suddenly.
How the archway and the voice and the shadow
seize the small triangle of my soul
violently, as in a silent film where the accompaniment
becomes a mad body
for the spirit's skipping images – abandoned homeland – miracle from
   which
we come back out alive. So here from there again I,
read it off the book of time,
my only time, as if in there is a fatal mistake of which
I cannot find the nature – or shape – or origin – I
pick up the infant and place it back again
to where I am a small reservoir of blood, twelve pounds of bone and
sinew and other matters – already condemned to this one soul –
which we are told weighs less than a feather, or as much
as four ounces when grown – as if I could travel, I back up
those arteries, up the precious liquid, across the field of methods,
   agonies,
astonishments – may I not squander the astonishments –
may I not mistakenly kill brother, sister – I
will sit once again so boldly at my beginning,
dark spot where one story does not yet become another,
and words, which have not yet come to me, will not yet try to tell
where each thing emerges, where it is heading,
and where the flow of tendency will shine
on its fast way downhill. And it will seem to me
that all this is legend,
one of those in which there is no way to look back
and yet you do, you pay for it, yes, but you do....

It was a hilltop town in the south in summer.
It was before I knew about knowing.
My mind ran everywhere and was completely still at the center.
And that did not feel uncomfortable.
A bird sang, it added itself to the shadow
under the archway.
I think from this distance
that I was happy.
I think from this distance.
I sat. It was before I knew walking.
Only my soul walked everywhere without weight.
Where the road sloped downhill there was disappearance.
Which was exactly what I imagined should happen.
Appearance and disappearance.
In my only life.
When my mother's voice got closer it had a body.
It had arms and they were holding something
that must have been a basket. My mind now
can go round her, come in front, and wrap her
as her arms wrapped that basket.
And it must have been wicker
because I see in the light the many lucent browns, the white tips,
as she steps out of the shadow
in which nothing but her hands and the front of her act of carrying
are visible. And when her body arrives
it is with the many lemons entirely struck, entirely taken, by sunshine,
which the heavy basket is still now carrying,
and her bright fingernails woven into each other,
and her face with its gaze searching for me,
gaze which felt like one of the bright things she was carrying
in front of herself, a new belly.
All I was to invent in this life is there in the wicker basket among
    the lemons
having come from below the horizon where the sound of the market
    rises
up into the private air in which she is moving,
where she is still a whole woman, and a willing woman,

and I hear what must be prices and names called out
of flowers and fruit and meat and live animals in small cages,
all from below us, at the bottom of the village, from that part
which is so comfortable to me which is invisible,
and in which everything has to be sold by noon.
I think that was the moment of my being given my name,
where I first heard the voices carrying the prices
as her face broke and its smile appeared bending down towards me
saying *there you are, there you are.*

The Bird on My Railing

From

the still wet iron of
my fire
escape's top
railing a truth is making this instant on our clock
open with a taut
unchirping un-
breaking note – a perfectly
released vowel traveling
the high branches across the way, between us and the
others, in their
apartments, and fog
lifting for sun before evaporation

begins. Someone
is born
somewhere
now. The
planet
suspends
like a streetlight
at night
in the quiet
galaxy.
Endurance
continues to be the secret of the tilled
ground we make
breath by breath. What
seed dear
lord are we we

think as we toss more of our living out
                              into the turning and turning,
                              our personal
dead cast always deeper into
                              the general dead
                              no matter how hard you try
                              to keep your
                              own your
known own – and gnarled remembering mossing over –
                              the tenderness a characteristic trait
                              elicits, the very thing you
                              hated, rising in you to
                              make you almost
                              unable to
                              speak –
– where *are* you? – the fields beyond the housing tract
                              still accepting rain
                              as these asphalted ones we've
                              sealed
cannot – so yes, look close, this right word on my railing
                              who knows no hate
                              no love
                              you can count on it,
no wrenching strangling guilt, no wish so terrible
                              one had said
                              otherwise just once in
                              time –
between one life and another what is it that
                              can really
                              exist – oh
                              nothing says this

awakeness – and look, you

          who might not believe this because
you are not seeing it with your own
          eyes: look:
          this light
          is moving
          across that flower on
          my sill
          at this exact
speed – right now – right here – now it is gone – yet go back up
          five lines it is
          still there I can't
          go back, it's
          gone,
          but you –
what is it you are

          seeing – see it again – a yellow
          daisy, the sun
          strafing the petals once
across, and the yellow, which could be a god why not,
          pulling itself up
          out of
shadow – so

          silent –
          and the patch of sunlight
          moves – and each word said in
          time after this is
          the subtraction we call
life-lived – this gold its center – and beyond it, still on
          the rail, this
          bird, a
          secret gift to
          me by the
          visible –

of which few in a life are

      given – and how
      when it opens its
      yellow beak in the glint-sun to
      let out song
      into the cold, it

lets out the note on a plume of

      steam
      lets out the
      visible heat of its
      inwardness

carrying a note – a note in

      a mist – a note-
      breath, breath-
      note – oh

cold spring – the white

      plume the size of a
      bird rises up with its own
      tail,
      feathering-out in

the directions,

      filled out by the next and the next-on
      note, until the whole
      shape of the
      song is wisped-
      up and

shuts,

      the singing
      shuts, the form
      complete, the breath-bird
      free to
      rise away into the young day and

not be –

Barry Hill

BOY WITH A PIGEON, 1944

In the palm of one hand
I can feel the soft weight of the bird
all its downiness of the kind
I had, once upon a time
on my cheek, my upper lip.

In my other hand its feathers quiver
then settle like a silk bow tie.

Blue sounds, blue sounds –
the bird colours my jacket
calls into my stiff throat.

Then we can't help but
bunch up a bit, tuck down
for a pin-pointed look.

NARCISSUS, 1950

*Sometimes when I've been staring too hard I've noticed that I
could see the circumference of my own eye*
                                    – Lucian Freud

What is it he sees?
Dove or dead monkey?

Or the dreaming lilies
still of his own hands?

If he could he would lift his head
hear the blue calls.

As it is
the water's frozen, holds him there.

Would that he could thread
his pullover right through

recover the half of his head
cut off by the ice.

Sadly (he knows, he knows)
he is crowned by each dry hair.

Geoffrey Hill

IV

Have I cloned Horace or reduced myself to
Weeping plasma? Never again so rightly,
Not again those *marvellous early poems*
            Lately acknowledged.

How the sea-lightning with a flash at hazard
Cleft the lanterned yard into pelting angles.
Had we been there, had you then turned towards me,
            By this remembered...

Yo, my sad love, clad in our dark declensions;
Never once naked to the other given;
Honey, milk, spices, of that night forgathered
            Lost in summation;

Mirrors fading where the bright-brutish roses
Held themselves royally akin their nature.
Berkeley could have granted us our existence
            Had we but known him.

Still suffices language its constitution;
Solipsist somehow must acknowledge this. Not
Quite enough said when what was said is nothing
            Granted recital.

Here is my good voice; you may well remember
Making up these things. It is what I do. Hark,
Love, how cross-rhythms are at stake to purpose
            From the beginning.

XXVIII

Broken that first kiss by the race to shelter,
Scratchy brisk rain irritable as tinder;
Hearing light thrum faintly the chords of laurel
        Taller than we were.

Fear to have already the direst choosing,
Sixty years spent as by procrastination.
Answer one question, this is all I need, so
        Speeding denial.

Ancient question haunting the Platonist: can
Spirit ransom body, and if so could I
Rise again in presence of your devoting
        Sorrow to sorrow?

Quick, is love's truth seriously immortal?
Would you might think so and not be this other
Finally known only through affirmation's
        Failing induction.

What though, wedded, we would have had annulment's
Consummation early, and though in darkness
I can see that glimmerous rim of folly
        Lave our condition,

Had we not so stumbled on grace, beloved,
In that chanced day brief as the sun's arising
Preternaturally without a shadow
        Cast in its presence.

Selima Hill

I used to have a tadpole I called Muriel
who'd look me in the eye as if to say

Give me back my pond, my lovely pondweed,
give me back my jellied palisades,

give me back whatever…then she died,
too small, too cold, too slimy to survive;

anyhow you too are much too small
and I'm ashamed to even have to look at you.

The Elephant is Much Too Big to Boogie

The elephant is much too big to boogie
and when I see him standing there like that
he makes me feel very nice and peaceful
like sobbing does when you sob and sob:
so ponderous and dim, he just stands there,
inert not with inertia but with love!
(The elephant is much too big to wink
but when he looks at me he almost does...)

Like summer days when nothing wants to move,
like wardrobes full of sleeping bags, the elephant
has gone to sleep without lying down,
he doesn't need to bother, he's got bones
specially made to double as a bed
for if you want to sleep standing up,
to close your eyes and let enormous planets
roll towards you like delicious buns.

Shortlisted Poems
The Felix Dennis Prize for Best First Collection

Loretta Collins Klobah

La Madonna Urbana

The dusk sky wore a corona of doves
        coasting over Los Dos Picos,
                the two pink, pointed breasts
      of la Iglesia de Dios Pentecostal
of Barrio Obrero in Santurce.
On this Isla encantada de Puerto Rico,
on La Calle Lima, is where it began,
    at an hour when Prospero's Tire Center
        had locked up (donde las gomas usadas
                no tienen garantía), and El Bohio Bar
      boomed its bachata bashment.

Maybe it started as a breeze
    off the water at the marina Los Laguneros,
        spiriting past the gutted Pinto jacked-up on concrete blocks,
           the burned out school bus. Maybe it was only vapour
                gliding past una gallina that ran in the road
                with its pollitos in La Buena Vista,
    eddying around an albino girl playing
    basketball in la cancha de un residencial,
two snakes of smoke drifting through a game of dominos in the park.

    Doña Doris, with a bag of cilantro, garlic, carrots, corn, peppers,
      and yautía from El Colmado Plaza Borinquén
        under her arm, was tired. She had come from the bus.
    She was walking home. She was the first to see the lips move.

There, at the back wall of the Colmado,
                where graffitero SKE and the FX TNB crew
had spray-painted the twelve-foot woman onto the wall, bust portrait
framed by a graffiti spell of petroglifos geométricos
        that called her spirit to the wall,
    Ske had painted her hair con el sabor del café del campo,

one highlighted strand at the forehead made of golden rum;
her dark brows and shadowed eyes sweet-talking and cockfighting;
her lips pressed closed, unsmiling;
her scooped blouse off-shoulder,
showing rhinestoned pink bra strap, abundant breasts.

Our Lady of Barrio Obrero, la señora profana, la madonna boricua,
la cabrona, la Gata,
this María, with street credentials painted just in front
of la Iglesia de Dios Pentecostal,
where, after storms, in shadowed night,
flooded streets turn into pools of sparkling light,
and the hard working campesinos de las clases empobrecidas
listen in their beds
to maracas of gun shots a las tres de la madrugada.
They lie in bed thinking that those shots
are not disparos al aire, but are meant to put bullets into someone
so that he will die before morning.

When the lips of the mural first moved a little, and the tongue darted out,
the faint sound was like the stir of a lady's Spanish fan,
a spider spinning in the inner nave of a guitar,
the butterfly kites of El Morro fluttering against the ocean air.
Then   quietly   came   *Ay,   Lei Lo Lai   Lei Lo Lai*

¡Ay, Señor! ¡Ave María! Doña Doris exclaimed and ran home to make love
to her husband three times in arabesque positions,
so she did not hear Our Lady
chanting the litany written on the wall of El Colmado:
Sandy, Cuajo, Goldo, Manuelito, Felipe, Glock, Chuola,
La bicha, Boricua grita paro nacional, el 15 de octubre,
las mujeres somos putas y puercas, William-n-Nadira,
Facundo Recordz, 100 X 35, Shakira pendeja,
¡Coño!

To Jorge in fishing galoshes and sweat-soused shirt,
carting his pole over his shoulder,

the lips whispered: *Busca para la vía de la esperanza.*
To Coraly with a boy child on her hip,
la Madonna Urbana sang Bob Marley's "No Woman No Cry".
To José in the sun, mending his hat with needle and thread on the curb:
Chivas Whiskey
To Alejandra skipping from the church in choir robe:
Tienes que ser una mujer con pantalones.
To Melba, community activist at 23 years old,
dueña of an ecotourism microempresa and defender
of the communities of El Caño Martin Peña:
Bendición   *Give thanks*

To Juanito, who limps barefooted on sun-melted asphalt
and drags his bad leg at the crossroads, our Legba,
whose open sore festering from knee to ankle has not healed in a year,
whose wound is unbandaged in the dusty street,
whose affliction is deep and wide
with ruffled edges of fat and meat around the opening,
whose leg we motorists have watched gradually turn colour
from trigueño to darkest black,
whose torn McDonald's cup we put money into day after day
because we know he is going to die soon,
sin velorio, sin baquiné,
and the money that we all endlessly work for will not stop that,
or the hour of our own death;
to Juanito, who, nonetheless is still singing
at our car windows as we wait for a stoplight
to turn the colour of the yankee dollar;
to Juanito who wears yellow rubber starfish earrings in both ears
and says, *Mamita, se ve bién, que linda eres*
and *Mira, tengo hambre;*

Juanito, the only one to notice
that sometimes Our Lady's hair also moves,
tossing like in a Clairol commercial,
making the air of Barrio Obrero taste of tamarindo;

to Juanito: *descansa.*

breathe.   never get weary yet.   alma, espíritu y cuerpo.

Graffiti Madonna cries out to us: *Pa'lante, Pa'lante, como un elefante.*

As the barrio sleeps, Our Lady of Providence and Juanito sing to us
with the voice of Ismael Rivera: *Las caras lindas, las caras lindas,*
las caras lindas de mi gente negra. Oyeme, pero que bonitas son, lindas son,
chulas son, bonitas son, lindas que son, lindas como tú verás, así son.

The last bus brings our men home from the night kitchens
while we feed her baby rice and Tabasco;
tie baby on the back with an African wrap,
and she sleeps. We watch British comedies
about bothersome, faded women, on the tele.
We break French and English trying
make sense of our lives, create our private pidgin.
On Saturdays we count coins, stroll Brixton market
to pick out yam, pepper, tomato, and a scrap of fish.
I buy pirate recordings of Stone Love Sound Clash.
When I'm leaving for good, going back to the Caribbean,
she brings me to her bedroom, where she unpacks *pagnes*
from home, Dutch Waxes, printed with flying fish
and stingray, and one green dress, fabric sheeny
with moon and star pattern when sun and shadow catches it.
Handpainted yellow cogs of colour wheel around the skirt;
uneven yellow rickrack adorns the neck.
A dress stitched in her Cote D'Ivoire. I will wear it
until the green fades to grey and patches of my skin
shine through thinning cloth. She brings out a pair
of embroidered satin high heels from Paris, impossibly
large for her feet or mine. She shows me how
she places paper in the toe to keep them in place.
I slide my feet in and try to raise myself
to that elevation. Feel the pinch of the paper.
Did she wear these shoes? They are beautiful.
The wadded paper, the way she helps me
hobble across the room to the mirror make them beautiful.
I will never wear them, but I place them in my bag,
promise to send American jeans and the hottest salsa music.
During the days, I have visited Notting Hill Carnival camps,
learned to play pan and sew parrot feathers, reasoned
with calypsonian Lord Cloak, drunk Carib with the sound-
lorry men and the women sewing spangles on spandex,
and interviewed a borough councillor who complained that

those West Indian riot-muckers pissed in his yard
and got too political with Carnival floats about Apartheid,
which went "like a swarm of bees" down the road.
At night, we have waited up together, both shy –
I, a guest in her home, a tramp picked up by her boarder
at an Africa Centre dance – grateful for a cold water flat
and kind lover to keep me warm. Her husband and my man, chefs,
work graveyard shifts and then ride the long night bus to Peckham.
Later, long after my good man goes off with an Italian gal
and I also travel to new, sadder romantic destinations,
the female friendship, of course, remains.
We exchange yearly photos of our daughters now and cards.
The yellow cogs on my worn-out green dress resemble
steel pan heads – I wear the music of London.
And I think of her and her warm cold water home.

Rhian Edwards

Skype

for B.L.H.

Now we have fallen by way
of a window, the motion
picture of a mouth, the faithful
companion of the voice,
staggered by a split
second.

Now we can only see the other
by looking away from the lens,
the voyeur conversing
conversing with its prey,
caressing your face
with a cursor.

Now we have come to a blur,
a pixelated mashing of atoms,
stock-stilled in vignette,
we re-focus the cynosure
with the fractious waking
of a bleary eye.

Now we are a screen, a sea
apart. Three thousand miles
as the crow flies, you lean
in for the kiss with only
the blue iris of the camera
to requite it.

Girl Meats Boy

The goose-necked fork and the cat-fanged knife
stood poles apart, like soldiering guards,
west and easting a world of plate
of petticoat white,
piled mole-mound high,
with the tatters of a man,
who had recently expired.

And my fingers thimbled fish cold steel,
eyes plump as fruit, with dripping pout,
my tongue unrolled red carpet-like,
as I ploughed and trowelled with tools and cut.

For plattered here was my better half,
my all-consuming light and dark,
who saw us better as separate halves.
A divorce I decreed with a slit apart.

And his white neck smirked an angry grin,
as the liquid poured in beetroot red.
Berry tears stained wall and tile,
as he stagger-waltzed, while draining dead.

He rag-doll slumped in a choir of pans,
where stew pots stooled his skull.
And all was mute 'cept weep of wound
ink-blotting troughs of metal.

I heaved the stew pots, bucket-brimmed,
slammed down on hobs and flame,
and fried the blood fat, pudding-black,
a macabre supper entertained.

Slabbed flat on ground, I sponged him down,
combed clean of smear and dirt.

I raked off hair with scrape and pluck
and skinned him pink and bald as birth.

I butchered limbs with rabid zeal
and knifed through muscled plums.
I ripped and gutted, as he did me,
and reduced this man to crumbs.

Ginger-root doused butter sweats
of garlic rocks and peppered dust,
I basted thigh and rump and breast,
and cooked him gold in a parsnipped nest.

His wave of hands slid down in soup
of mushroom nutmeg milk,
so dab of hand and finger-tickle
could brush my lips with each spooned gulp.

I jellied thoughts in pickle sour,
soused face in stew of onions.
I parched his ears to biscuit bread,
crisped nose to pencil shavings.

I cured his heart, I syruped it sweet,
cake-baked in cream and cherries.
My menyou done, I throned to dine,
claw-pawed at the ash grey cutlery.

Lips fell apart for kiss of you,
bled puddled spit for scraps of you,
gouged cheeks of meat to feast on you,
tore threads of flesh in teeth of you,
licked marrow, bone and pulp of you,
let belly swell with fat of you,
pigged pregnant with the pith of you,
gut, liver, spleen digesting you,
my newborn blood absorbing you,

my pulse, my veins, heart pumping you.
No flies on you, no worms in you,
no scavenge bait, no urn of you.

From liver to liver,
heart to heart
blood to blood.

This woman, she made
a meal of you.

Lucy Hamilton

LANDMARKS & BOUNDARIES

Soon I am outside the city, beyond the formality of Versailles and the strictures of St. Cyr. I have passed Trappes and am heading out into open countryside where my journey becomes easier through fields and sleeping villages. A dog barks. Owls gaze down from the branches of darkly-silhouetted trees. I sense their watchful presence. On and on I travel, taking long strides across valleys, streams, fallen trees. Nothing can stop me until at last the village comes into view. The Square is deserted, the petrol-sign swinging stiffly in the wind. The house is changed but it is the house and I know he is inside.

A golden light radiates under the door. Utter silence as I turn the knob. Gradually my eyes adjust. The room is electric with static and feathers that glide and spiral like a blizzard of snow-flakes. Then I see their bodies. The bed is a trampoline as they bounce entwined, their god-like beauty brushed by a ballet of swans.

I shut the door softly and leave for ever. My return to the city is difficult and confused for all the landmarks have changed. I stray into alien territory where the earth is scorched a deep terracotta-red and the isolation is primordial. Should I go forward or back? I retrace my steps, a stranger to myself. At last, stopping to rest and get my bearings, I notice an owl perched on a fence-post and tentatively ask him how long and far my journey will take me. With a detached expression he considers, blinking and ruffling a feather. I understand his reply. It is nothing less than I expected.

THE CHAIR

Flew through the window when I wasn't watching. The boy outside the door says it happened by magic or accident. Believing magic and knowing accident I extract a promise and the boy walks home to the Estate. In the Head's Office the Head, the Head of Year and the Head of Faculty speak sternly. You mean to say you *trust* him? they exclaim. I do not mention magic. Next morning the boy is prompt. The Head scratches his head.

Sam Riviere

FALL IN LOVE ALL OVER AGAIN

much against everyone's advice
I have decided to live the life
I want to read about and write it
not by visiting the graves of authors
or moving to london to hear
in my sleep its gothic lullaby
not by going for coastal walks
or being from the north and lathing
every line as an approach it's
way outmoded I run a bath turn
off the lights I think only of
lathering the pale arms of my wife
for now a girl who dreads weekends
then I guess I might as well teach
squandering so as not to squander
this marvellous opportunity right?

BUFFERING 15%

you aren't thinking clearly as you enter the bank
on the day leslie nielson dies
the coldest december 'in living memory'
mark's badge reads
'have a good time all the time'
maybe you should think about getting a motto
maybe you should think about painting the fridge blue again
maybe then you'd feel less like the shape of a person
suggested by the fall of light on a bookcase
you find you're thinking a lot about your friend the monk
who won't share with you his secret
to be sure he is a very complex gentleman
but hardly deep even if he can <u>burn leaves</u>
<u>with nothing but the power of his mind</u>
he is a remorseless self-publicist
maybe that's his secret
or his secret is he doesn't have one
he claims to remember where he buried
a live beetle in a matchbox
but afflicted as you are with awful memories
you're not sure you believe him
filling out the paying-in slip is difficult
maybe you should stop growing your fingernails
'shhh' he went this morning
pretending to be listening

Jacob Sam-La Rose

After Lazerdrome, McDonalds, Peckham Rye

> *What's clear, now, is / that there was music, that it's lasted, that it /*
> *doesn't matter whether a player played it, / or whether it just played itself,*
> *that it still is / playing, / that at least two gods exist...*
>   Abdulah Sidran, 'A Dispute About God'

where I say goodbye to south-east London for the next 3 years
a gaggle of us   still damp   spilling in from the night before

early flock for a Sunday   six or seven A.M.   sleepless
drowning in light and all this quiet   after all that sweat
and darkness   all that flighty noise

this is the year one of the guys says music is the one thing
that won't ever let him down   that music is his religion

the year we're stopped and searched because we
fit the description   the year jungle music passes
out of fashion   stripped down

to naked beat and bass   and we club together   to dance
alone   in the dark   let the music play us   meat and bone

let music fill the empty spaces   rhythm in wads and scads
scattershot   crashing   wall to wall   to be baptised
by filtered drums   pressed snares and swollen b-lines

be baptised by city songs   urban hymns   seamless
sound   a brimming sea of sound   poured out

from towering speaker stacks   this is the year we stand
close enough   to feel the music   rise   its wing-beats
on our faces   drawing salt from our skin   released

then morning   small fries and a strawberry milkshake
counting coins for the cab back   sitting around a table

slouching in moulded seats   drowning in silence
light-headed   leavened   waiting
for the right moment to move

awake for too long   ears
still ringing   drum-drunk

eyes still adjusting to the light
a weight coming down

How to be Gravity

Be a mammy.

Fleshy arms unwilling to let anything go
and always someone fighting your grip,
trying
         to muster enough speed to escape you.

Enforce the rules with the palm of your hand.
Moonlight as death
                    or a jealous god.

Put heaven and hell in their place.

Know that there are more intimate places
to hook your anchors
than flesh or bone.

There's a part of everyone
that will always escape you
                         at the end.

Until then, pull everything
                 down,
         down,
down.

Shortlisted Poems
The Forward Prize for Best Single Poem

Marilyn Hacker

Fugue on a Line of Amr bin M'ad Yakrib

ذهب الذي أحبّهم و بقيتُ مثل السيف فرداً

Those whom I love have gone
And I remain, like a sword, alone.

Gone, yes, or going, determination hardens
Into a self-destructive stubbornness.

What melody will resonate its presence
If you play the same old self-reflective chord alone?

Someone who wrote, 'Never to lose you again'
Moved, sent no message with a new address

And in that memory there is a mountain,
Above it, a reddish hawk that swooped and soared alone.

Who held a sword and said that he resembled
A sword, in his solitude was nothing less.

Between the old man and the steely angel,
A sleep-drunk intern holding down the ward alone.

The word-root's there, you look into the branches'
cadence and contexts you can only guess.

Translating from a slow-emerging language
Resembles dialogue, and I'm less bored, alone.

Though it's a doubled blade to be a weapon
And turn yourself onto your own distress.

Silent among her servants, Balqis riding
Back toward her queendom praised the Lord alone.

If the beloved asked, what would you wish of me?
That without my asking, you would answer 'Yes'.

The glass of wine not offered to the green-eyed stranger,
The nightly second glass of wine I poured alone.

John Kinsella

MEA CULPA: CLEANING THE GUTTERS

Not quite believing that rain would come
in thimblefuls never mind buckets, pre-
dawn deluge, cracking of the skies
with essence of light made out of absolute
darkness, took me unawares. I'd learnt
not to believe in forecasts, to doubt
even the particular movements of birds.

Not quite believing that rain would come
I'd left cleaning the gutters, while lamenting
the emptying of the Great Tank down to its final
rung, or reaching its echo full-blown, grown
to fill an emptiness, replete with sound,
those final drops of silt and leaves that settle
having found their way through pipes to brew.

Not quite believing that rain would come
I had to wait until the last gasp of thunder,
brace the ladder, and work my way around the house,
circumnavigate and excavate the gutters: black silage
scooped and flopped to the ground – inky and indelible
even on sand. And then down to the trap to release
the filth, and scouring even the Great Tank's top itself.

Not quite believing that the rain would come
I lose time and water and watch taps flow brown.
Mea culpa, Thomas the Doubter, and whatever negative
affirmations run through my head. Cut by the tin roof,
I have only one hand free to revise what's been
hastily done: bloody hand dangling at my side,
useless and polluting as I waver near rain and sky.

Michael Longley

You are dying. Why do we fight?
You find my first published poem –
'Not worth the paper it's printed on,'
You say. *She gave him marigolds* –

You are dying. 'They've cut out my
Wheesht – I have to sit down
To *wheesht* – like a woman' –
Marigolds *the colour of autumn* –

I need to hitchhike to Dublin
For Trinity Term. 'I'll take you
Part of the way,' you say,
'And we can talk if you like.'

And we talk and talk as though
We know we are just in time.
'A little bit further,' you say
Again and again, and in pain.

A few miles from Drogheda
You turn the car. We say goodbye
And you drive away slowly
Towards Belfast and your death.

To keep in his cold room. Look
At me now on the Newry Road
Standing beside my rucksack. Och,
Daddy, look in your driving mirror.

Denise Riley

A PART SONG

i

You principle of song, what are you *for* now
Perking up under any spasmodic light
To trot out your shadowed warblings?

Mince, slight pillar. And sleek down
Your furriness. Slim as a whippy wire
Shall be your hope, and ultraflexible.

Flap thinly, sheet of beaten tin
That won't affectionately plump up
More cushioned and receptive lays.

But little song, don't so instruct yourself
For none are hanging around to hear you.
They have gone bustling or stumbling well away.

ii

What is the first duty of a mother to a child?
At least to keep the wretched thing alive – Band
Of fierce cicadas, stop this shrilling.

My daughter lightly leaves our house.
The thought rears up: *fix in your mind this*
Maybe final glimpse of her. Yes, lightning could.

I make this note of dread, I register it.
Neither my note nor my critique of it
Will save us one iota. I know it. And.

iii

Maybe a retouched photograph or memory,
This beaming one with his striped snake-belt

45

And eczema scabs, but either way it's framed
Glassed in, breathed hard on, and curated.
It's odd how boys live so much in their knees.
Then both of us had nothing. You lacked guile
And were transparent, easy, which felt natural.

    iv

Each child gets cannibalised by its years.
It was a man who died, and in him died
The large-eyed boy, then the teen peacock
In the unremarked placid self-devouring
That makes up being alive. But all at once
Those natural overlaps got cut, then shuffled
Tight in a block, their layers patted square.

    v

It's late. And it always will be late.
Your small monument's atop its hillock
Set with pennants that slap, slap, over the soil.
Here's a denatured thing, whose one eye rummages
Into the mound, her other eye swivelled straight up:
A short while only, then I come, she carols – but is only
A fat-lot-of-good mother with a pointless alibi: 'I didn't
Know.' Yet might there still be some part for me
To play upon this lovely earth? Say. Or
Say *No*, earth at my inner ear.

    vi

A wardrobe gapes, a mourner tries
Her several styles of howling-guise:

You'd rather not, yet you must go
Briskly around on beaming show.

A soft black gown with pearl corsage
Won't assuage your smashed ménage.

It suits you as you are so pale.
Still, do not get that saffron veil.

Your dead don't want you lying flat.
There'll soon be time enough for that.

vii

Oh my dead son you daft bugger
This is one glum mum. Come home I tell you
And end this tasteless melodrama – quit
Playing dead at all, by now it's well beyond
A joke, but your humour never got cruel
Like this. Give over, you indifferent lad,
Take pity on your two bruised sisters. For
Didn't we love you. As we do. But by now
We're bored with our unproductive love,
And infinitely more bored by your staying dead
Which can hardly interest you much, either.

viii

Here I sit poleaxed, stunned by your vanishing
As you practise your charm in the underworld
Airily flirting with Persephone. Not *so hard
To imagine* what her mother *had gone through*
To be ferreting around those dark sweet halls.

ix

They'd sworn to stay for ever but they went
Or else I went – then concentrated hard
On the puzzle of what it ever truly *meant*
For someone to be here then, just like that
To not. Training in mild loss was useless
Given the final thing. And me lamentably
Slow to 'take it in' – far better toss it out,
How should I take in such a bad idea. No,
I'll stick it out instead for presence. If my
Exquisite hope can wrench you right back
Here, resigned boy, do let it as I'm waiting.

x

I can't get sold on reincarnating you
As those bloody 'gentle showers of rain'
Or in 'fields of ripening grain' – oooh
Anodyne – nor yet on shadowing you
In the hope of eventually pinpointing
You bemused among the *flocking souls*
Clustered like bats, as all thronged gibbering
Dusk-veiled – nor in modern creepiness.
Lighthearted presence, be bodied forth
Straightforwardly. Lounge again under
The sturdy sun you'd loved to bake in.
Even ten seconds' worth of a sighting
Of you would help me get through
This better. With a camera running.

xi

Ardent bee, still you go blundering
With downy saddlebags stuffed tight
All over the fuchsia's drop earrings.
I'll cry 'Oh bee!' to you, instead –
Since my own dead, apostrophised,
Keep mute as this clear garnet glaze
You're bumping into. Blind diligence,
Bee, or idiocy – this banging on and on
Against such shiny crimson unresponse.

xii

Outgoing soul, I try to catch
You calling over the distances
Though your voice is echoey,

Maybe tuned out by the noise
Rolling through me – or is it
You orchestrating that now,

Who'd laugh at the thought
Of me being sung in by you
And being kindly dictated to.

It's not like hearing you live was.
It is what you're saying in me
Of what is left, gaily affirming.

xiii
Flat on a cliff I inch toward its edge
Then scrutinise the chopped-up sea
Where gannets' ivory helmet skulls
Crash down in tiny plumes of white
To vivify the languid afternoon –
Pressed round my fingertips are spikes
And papery calyx frills of fading thrift
That men call sea pinks – so I can take
A studied joy in natural separateness.
And I shan't fabricate some nodding:
'She's off again somewhere, a good sign
By now, she must have got over it.'

xiv
Dun blur of this evening's lurch to
Eventual navy night. Yet another
Night, day, night over and over.
I so want to join you.

xv
The flaws in suicide are clear
Apart from causing bother
To those alive who hold us dear
We could miss one another
We might be trapped eternally
Oblivious to each other
One crying *Where are you, my child*
The other calling *Mother*.

xvi

Dead, keep me company
That sears like titanium
Compacted in the pale
Blaze of living on alone.

xvii

Suspended in unsparing light
The sloping gull arrests its curl
The glassy sea is hardened waves
Its waters lean through shining air
Yet never crash but hold their arc
Hung rigidly in glaucous ropes
Muscled and gleaming. All that
Should flow is sealed, is poised
In implacable stillness. Joined in
Non-time and halted in free fall.

xviii

It's all a resurrection song.
Would it ever be got right
The dead could rush home
Keen to press their chinos.

xix

She do the bereaved in different voices
For the point of this address is to prod
And shepherd you back within range
Of my strained ears; extort your reply
By finding any device to hack through
The thickening shades to you, you now
Strangely unresponsive son, who were
Such reliably kind and easy company,
Won't you be summoned up once more
By my prancing and writhing in a dozen
Mawkish modes of reedy piping to you
– Still no? Then let me rest, my dear.

XX

My sisters and my mother
Weep dark tears for me
I drift as lightest ashes
Under a southern sea

O let me be, my mother
In no unquiet grave
My bone-dust is faint coral
Under the fretful wave

Greta Stoddart

Deep Sea Diver

There's a field inside my head.
It's dark and flat and a moon

hangs above it in whose silvery
negative light nothing appears to live.

It's very mysterious and simple,
on a different planet

to the one outside my window
that moves and is manifold:

each one of the tens of millions of blades of grass
shivers in its singularity;

one sheep's crusty underwool is home
to a greenbottle settling down to lay
her two hundred and fifty possibilities

while another stares out
of the glazed globe of an eye
not unlike a man who's lost his mind
but found there cause instead
to be vaguely, dully, afraid of everything.

And beneath the sheep
and field and flattened buttercups

miles and mile beneath,
all is shift and shale,
burn and boil:

old underearth
unseeable, unexplorable;

who scrambles through your soft weak rock,
who swims through your molten ocean,
what holds court at the centre
of your solid iron ball the size of the moon?

Once I plumbed down
level by level

into the sea,
into the realm

of the falling-debris,
dead and dying-fish-eating creatures

into the pitch black frigid waters
and blind long-tentacled things;

down among the deepwater canyons I went
and still nowhere near was I

to the outer core
of the earth's interior,
its massive indoors

when I saw hanging there
a sole, or flounder

a self never before seen – never before a self

but one who remained unchanged
in the bright beam of my look
(though something may have gone through it
like the mildest electric shock)

and I rose to the surface
like one who had only that to do

where slowly over the years
all that I held dear came loose

and I took to wandering the fields

that covered the earth
like so many soft individual dressings

and I lay down on one
and looked up at the sky

where I saw a fish hanging
in the black, where I saw a moon.

Highly Commended Poems

2012

Emily Berry

LETTER TO HUSBAND

Dearest husband Beloved husband Most respected,
missed and righteous husband Dear treasured, absent
husband Dear unimaginable piece of husband
Dear husband of the moon, it has been six months since I
Dear much lamented distant husband, my champing heart
forgives you please come. In a long
undergrowth of wanting I creep at night the sea is a dark room
I called and called These white corridors are not
free from longing Dear postman Dear night-time, dear
dark mouth hovering over me Dear knee bones
dear palms, dear faithful body I have wants

Husband – Speech is a dark stain spreading
I have no telephone No one will give me a telephone
I lost your voice in dark places it is written
over and over that please come.
A scribble is the way a heartbeat is told Dearest serrated
husband. My heartscribbles your name. My mouth
scribbles: I have cried your name in every
possible colour I have given you my proud desperate
undeviating wish over and over and over: Sweetheart, please come

Ruth Bidgood

Joy

At the farm down the road
I remember a sheepdog, lugubrious Joy,
who pensioned off spent her mournful days
drooping in the middle of the road,
meeting with equal indifference
the soothing words of strangers
and the chance of crushing death.

A day came when Joy
disappeared; cars no longer slowed
to dodge the melancholy obstacle.
I couldn't bring myself to ask
Where's Joy?, feeling that while
the question wasn't put,
wasn't answered, I could still
picture her lurking sombrely
in some nook of a barn, even
welcomed inside to eke out
her sad and shortening days
by the stove, or in summer
on the porch mat. It was long
before I accepted the certainty
that never again would Joy's
ineffable dreariness lend
a dark spice to the blandest of days.

Kate Bingham

OPEN

The sound of the place was the sound of summer air –
on holiday the same place every year
it was a field or tree or temperature
I never thought to hear and never heard

until the time I took a boy up there
and closed his eyes and with his open ear
my prickled lips and cheeks and forehead saw
behind the sun the singing of a bird.

If I had never listened to a heart
till then, I would have felt the sudden shame
and same unfolding lunatic delight

I felt beneath that fluttering spark in flight,
discovering the lark and in its name
a song that had been with me from the start.

Sean Borodale

I keep the queen, she is long in my hand,
her legs slightly pliant;
folded, dropped down, wings flat
that flew her mating flight
to the sun and back, full of spermatozoa, dronesong.
She was made mechanically ecstatic.
I magnify what she is, magnify her skews and centres.
How downy she is, fur like a fox's greyness, like a thistle's mane.
Wings perfect, abdomen subtle in shades of brittle;
her rear legs are big in the lens;
feet like hung anchors are hooks for staying on cell-rims.
Veins in her wings are a rootwork of rivers,
all echo and interlace. This is her face, compound eye.
I look at the slope of her head, the mouth's proboscis;
her thin tongue piercing is pink as cut flesh, flash glass.
Some hairs feather and split below the head.
Those eyes are like castanets, cast nets;
woman all feral and ironwork, I slip
under the framework, into the subtle.
The wing is jointed at the black leather shoulder.
I wear it, I am soft to stroke, the lower blade fans.
Third generation queen of our stock,
you fall as I turn. I hold your hunchback;
a carcase of lightness, no grief, part animal, part flower.

Dan Burt

SLOWLY SOUNDS THE BELL

> *Nunc lento sonitu dicunt, morieris.*
> *Now this bell tolling softly for another,*
> *says to me, Thou must die.*
> > Donne, Meditation XVII

A midnight ring from half a world away
Tolls my only brother's sudden death.
Line dead, handset re-cradled, sleep returns;
I wake to find bedclothes scarcely messed.

We long were distant islands to each other –
I stood Esau to his Jacob as a boy,
My fields the sea, his tents the libraries –
DNA proved inadhesive, no gene
Sutured the rifts between us, and the news
Was less vexing than a tree fall in my garden.

We hope for more: a foetal element
Feeding fondness for our kin, a shared
Enzyme sealing first cousins best of friends,
From propinquity Gileadan balm.

But boyhood hatred, dumb decades apart,
Change blood to water, degauss genealogies;
Abel becomes Cain's pathogen. A shrug
In the cell metastasises through
Isolate null points of the tribe into
Skull paddies and black snow in June.

Religious tapestries woven from old deities
Cannot conceal trenches we dig between us:
Ancestral chemistry stands hooded on
The scaffold, testing trap and rope for all.

It is the face on the school run who mouths
'Hello', a torso hunched on the next bar stool
Twice a week, a high school sweetheart back,
A man selling ceramics I collect
Dying of AIDS, whose curfews heave the clapper
Summoning tears, the shiver in the neck.

Jennifer Clarvoe

THAT WAY

It's wrong for him to hit her in that way
across the face – completely wrong. That way
madness lies. When Malkovich hits Kidman
in Campion's *Portrait of a Lady*, man
turns beast. But Gilbert Osmond is a beast
to Isabel when he is least a beast,
when he refuses to display his rage
at her; he is most cruel when his rage
is coldest, softest, quietest – and she
cannot fight back, can hardly even speak
or move. His tone, when he at last does speak,
is grave, sincere, with all the subtlety
of the subtlest threads that tether her, subtlety
so much more cruel than outright violence –
that's why it's wrong, that outright violence.
If he had hit her, that would let her go –
it would explode in her and let her go.
When he hauls off and hits her he is changed
just as surely as Lycaon is changed
into a wolf by the force of his emotion,
and Actaeon to a deer by *his* emotion –
choked with rage the tyrant cannot speak,
the breathless, panicked victim cannot speak –
the body registers rage and fear past words –
and Isabel and Osmond are past words,
where words can't reach, about to force the story
to the bursting point: this is the story
that tells us, now that violence exists,
it exists the way the real body exists –
to free us from the things we cannot say –
the body exists to free us in that way.

John Clegg

MERMAIDS

We'd explode from the change in pressure
before we saw daylight, and anyway
evolution has sheathed our eyes as dead ends.
We live by taste, which is really smell;
we taste what's diffused in water
and sense the direction. Carcasses mostly.

We've kept a vague idea of our shape:
wing-spindles propelling us forward,
armoured backplate, excretory organs.
But sex is a mystery. Our best guess
has males as the krill-like specks
which winkle, sometimes, under our chitin.

We sing to each other in pheromone, never
certain how message matches to sender.
Sometimes we taste our long past's echo.
We cultivate theories on the existence
of dry land, spin theologies of loneliness. We hang
translucent in love's deepwater trenches.

Anne Cluysenaar

Moon

for Walt

Nothing of Earth shows
tonight but the tips of the forest
against a bright white moon
almost full, half risen.

When our forebears saw something like this
they must have wondered how light,
such light, could exist in such darkness.
As for us, we know. And our knowledge

tells how the sun whirls us round,
how the planet's exploded side
was rounded off, like this globe
itself, by the rush of gravity.

A fast wind, silently high,
drives cloud across, and the tree-tops
topple. We ourselves seem
to be moving. And we are, we are!

All at once, it is good to stand
unappalled together. To find that to be,
just here, enjoying all this,
is a thing human minds can do.

Julia Copus

This is the poem in which I have not left you.
The doors of the Green Dragon are not bolted
behind our backs; the pink-faced landlady
(may she be blessed) has not abandoned us
to the unseasonable cold, that March
evening of your thirty-seventh year.
In the gloom that hangs over South Street, in the quiet
made of the humming of streetlights and the moon,
the horn from a distant freight train does not sound;
I do not turn – my tongue is tied, my hands –
whatever there is to say is left unsaid.
And since I dare not speak, nothing transpires:
the street, in the moments after, does not shrink
to the slam of a door, the flare of an engine, you
suddenly elsewhere, you imagined, gone,
but seen, still seen (the night stretching between us),
cursing the fog on the Blackdowns, curving, finally,
into the narrow driveway of the cottage.

Our cottage, I meant to say, with its yellow walls,
its broken gate – I might have forgotten those,
and the fields and the light, were it not for the fact
that this is the poem in which we do not part,
but lie like lovers, one of whom is sleeping,
my head, as always, nearest the leaky window
through which the old sounds reach me – rain in the trees,
a gust of wind, a tipper truck, a siren
threading its way through the dark (but you'll not wake;
your ears are shut, you won't admit a thing).
Then further off, after the rain is done,
the voice of the redstart calling *do it, do it!*,
calling from the smallest tree in the garden.

Carol Ann Duffy

WATER

Your last word was *water*,
which I poured in a hospice plastic cup, held
to your lips – your small sip, half-smile, sigh –
then, in the chair beside you,
                                   fell asleep.

Fell asleep for three lost hours,
only to waken, thirsty, hear then see
a magpie warn in a bush outside –
dawn so soon – and swallow from your still-full cup.

Water. The times I'd call as a child
for a drink, till you'd come, sit on the edge
of the bed in the dark, holding my hand,
just as we held hands now and you died.

A good last word.
                        Nights since I've cried, but gone
to my own child's side with a drink, watched
her gulp it down then sleep. *Water.*
What a mother brings
                                   through darkness still
to her parched daughter.

Helen Dunmore

The Malarkey

Why did you tell them to be quiet
and sit up straight until you came back?
The malarkey would have led you to them.

You go from one parked car to another
and peer through the misted windows
before checking the registration.

Your pocket bulges. You've bought them sweets
but the mist is on the inside of the windows.
How many children are breathing?

The malarkey's over in the back of the car.
The day is over outside the windows.
No street light has come on.

You fed them cockles soused in vinegar,
you took them on the machines.
You looked away just once.

You looked away just once
as you leaned on the chip-shop counter,
and forty years were gone.

You have been telling them for ever
Stop that malarkey in the back there!
Now they have gone and done it.
Is that mist, or water with breath in it?

Paul Durcan

SUNNY HILL
after Veronica Bolay

Painting quickly at the beginning of the twenty-first century
On the north-west coast of Europe,
She gets up with the sun at 4.30 a.m.
Not knowing if anything – anything? – lies ahead.

The sun never rises the same way twice
On the hill in front of her and she knows
That this morning she will have to paint more quickly
Than any morning ever before in her life.

How on earth can she do it? Is it possible?
All those zillions of shades of the "high yellow note",
Montbretia-in-the-sky-with-fuchsia!
A symphonic fireworks display of sunniness.

Then she sees the gate at the bottom of the sky
As if for the first time – the same islanded gate in the bog
She has been looking at for fifty years –
The gate marooned in spite of its two green roads.

Seeing how she has always failed the gate
She wants to throw herself down in the gateway
And cry out to the gate – "Father! Mother!"
She who is sick unto death of nostalgia.

"O my little grey six-barred gate," she whispers,
Before squeezing tubes of red pigment on to canvas
And painting the grey gate red –
The goldenest red of all black reds.

But all that having been done
Down across the bottom of the canvas,
With what is she to fill up the empty canvas above?
All that sky, all that spilt sunlight?

Not even a pathologist's microscope could depict
Such intricate detail as do her brushes and knives
Of the dawn sky's extra-adrenal paraganglia –
The sky's tumours as a gold mosaic.

Away with her brushes! Away with her knives!
She throws herself face-down on the blue grass.
Facing her own oblivion in the glory of her death
Never has she been so delighted to be who she is.

14 July 2009

Helen Farish

A Night in at Nohant

*(One player shuffles a pack of homemade cards, picks a musical key;
the player opposite must describe the key using words or phrases.
Advanced players only: keys can be replaced with single notes.)*

A minor – rain, mansard roofs,
the heart a bedraggled stray animal
looking at the turning of wheels,
the silk button you recall
your mother stitching onto the pleat
of a blue coat with grey lining.

C major – blocks of colour: the sea,
a field, kittens, a child, a daffodil.

E flat major – white china plates,
to be the last of a party on its way
to the river, the seed-heavy heads
of grasses brushed by skirts, notes
like butter left in a warm dish.

B – on a faded wall of thin-sky blue, the trembling
reflection of the smallest pane in the house,
the late low sun netted in a mesh of leaves.

F sharp – snow-melt filling the grooves
of carriage wheels as you walk along
rue Rivoli at dusk; the moss which spends
its winter covering the arm of a stone seat;
that woman you remember shaking a red rug
from the first floor window of a white house
in a city you've forgotten or confuse.

Paul Farley

THE POWER

Forget all of that end-of-the-pier
palm-reading stuff. Picture a seaside town
in your head. Start from its salt-wrack-rotten smells
and raise the lid of the world to change the light,
then go as far as you want: the ornament
of a promenade, the brilliant greys of gulls,
the weak grip of a crane in the arcades
you've built, ballrooms to come alive at night,
then a million-starling roost, an opulent
crumbling like cake icing...
                                        Now, bring it down
in the kind of fire that flows along ceilings,
that knows the spectral blues; that always starts
in donut fryers or boardwalk kindling
in the dead hour before dawn, that leaves pilings
marooned by mindless tides, that sends a plume
of black smoke high enough to stain the halls
of clouds. Now look around your tiny room
and tell me that you haven't got the power.

James Fenton

AT THE KERB
i.m. Mick Imlah

Grief to bestow, where once they bestowed their beauty,
Who are these mourners processing to the grave,
Each bearing a history like a precious ointment
And tender on their sleeves the wounds of love?

Brutal disease has numbered him a victim,
As if some unmarked car had appeared one day
And snatched him off to torture and confinement,
Then dumped him by the kerbside and sped away;

As if they stooped now at the kerb to lift the body,
As if they broke the jars and unguent flowed,
Flowed down the sleeves and wounds, ran down the kerbstones,
Grief to bestow what beauty once bestowed.

Philip Gross

NOT SAYING

How plain
can I say it
yet mean
what I say,

how to straiten
mere abundance
into generosity,

how to pass
through the I
of the needling ache
to meet you

in a place no longer there maybe

except that now you could
be anybody
out beyond words beyond
most memory

and I don't mean 'anybody
else', I mean I could
be you, you could be me

even 'love' is a difficult word
for something plainer
like the not-saying
when you see me find

and take your soiled secreted laundry

like the seeing you see
like the touching your hand
you mine
as slightly as a child's

last moment before
their first teeter upright
like a hint

of the tremendous
silent language
we may some day speak
or be?

Geoff Hattersley

No One Knows Why

Old dogs in the garden, barking
Barking all night, into morning

Turning slightly in a cool breeze
A man on the end of a rope

Barking all night, into morning
Turning slightly in a cool breeze

Calmly tied the rope to a beam
Had to get something right for once

Last fish 'n' chips supper, the final cigarette
Snapshots spread out on the table

Had to get something right for once
Calmly tied the rope to a beam

He jumped through the trap door
Meant to smile but he sobbed

Snapshots spread out on the table
Last fish 'n' chips supper, the final cigarette

He jumped through the trap door
A man on the end of a rope

Meant to smile but he sobbed
Old dogs in the garden, barking

Oli Hazzard

FOUR LANDSCAPES

1.

Outside in the fields it is raining
with the sound of plastic bags uncrumpling
in a palm cupped around an ear
pointed towards this coffee-coloured sea
across which a number of small boats sail
as if the dangers were no longer rational
but formed only an embarrassing example
of what hesitancies should never cross
the vellum on a distant apostle's desk.

2.

Absorbed by the city's motheaten cube
I am learning about the history of Libya
the inbox choking itself with charity junk
thick miles of sunlight unrolled
an abandoned blueprint curling up on its tube
I am terrific and unable to concentrate
on the calibre of hesitation that characterises
what I imagine to be the space across which I
distinguish between thinking and speaking.

3.

This being some kind of slow journey
or scenic route taking in all the sights of the local
countryside the spasm of the coastal
road displaying moments between the shrill
trees full of insects the calculable distance
of the land point shanking the sea and birds

hanging as though caught on some tether
we can relax into deep distances between speaking
floating words cut adrift from words.

4.

Clouds pull apart with a doughy lightness
as we stumble out into open fields
where birds form then dissolve in the tentings
of spreathed sunlight and garbled
scrawls are lifted from the saffron-spatter
scratching out some other walker's tread
cuffs of frost wilt the edges of splayed leaves
oscitant voices dye the silence rust
the sound of blood mizzling in the lull.

David Herd

3 Notes Towards a Love Song

1

The world is feral today and still
There is much between us
This dumb old November weather
Consequential, nothing but itself.
The land before us so thickly clothed already,
This is objectively a love song,
Standing us opposite
Densely manufactured
By slow degree.

2

Feral, like a love song.
The shy old planet has nothing to say to us this morning.
Dumb,
Consequential,
Manufactured old
Earth.

Nothing to say –
Maybe we should get on with it,
Objectively, a love song,
Allow things,
Comrade,
To be difficult between us.

3

Camarade, this morning,
Things have this shy way of happening,
So that if we should speak

It is barely established
Either one of us belongs

In this weather we have
Making all things difficult
So that even your being here is a blessing
In these several senses which pass into each other
Showing in the circumstances
What the world might hold.

Establishing
There is much between us
As dumb old November plays itself out
And we stand opposite contemplating the distance
By some slow degree,
Forage quietly in each other's language
Manufacturing a love song

Objectively,
Comrade,
Among trees.

Jane Hirshfield

The Supple Deer

The quiet opening
between fence strands
perhaps eighteen inches.

Antlers to hind hooves,
four feet off the ground,
the deer poured through.

No tuft of the coarse white belly hair left behind.

I don't know how a stag turns
into a stream, an arc of water.
I have never felt such accurate envy.

Not of the deer:

To be that porous, to have such largeness pass through me.

Julith Jedamus

BARN BURNING, FALL RIVER, WISCONSIN, JULY 1966

Back of the house, past hickory trees and mangled sheets,
stood the barn where my mother swung above the threshing floor,
dared by her brothers, scared by the freight-train rush of air
slamming her chest, her rope-burned hands losing their purchase

as she flew through the dark and fell into my arms. Only in dreams
can I save her like this – her thinness through gingham,
her jujube breath. We lie for years and years as doves moan
in rafters for all she lost: the hushed disasters and alarms.

Through wide-swung doors she led me though the crowd:
the whole town of Fall River gathered there in the July forenoon
to watch the burning of the barn. It was gone by the midday siren.
Boys threw chairs onto its smoldering shade.

Was it progress of a kind to stand with her at childhood's edge,
on fresh asphalt, by the new aluminum garage?
No bats, no memories, no ropes to test her courage –
our Ektachrome smiles gleam like her green crowned Dodge.

Mimi Khalvati

The Swarm

Snow was literally swarming round the streetlamp like gnats.
The closer they came, the larger they grew, snow-gnats, snow-bees,

and in my snood, smoking in the snow, I watched them.
Everyone else was behind the door, I could hear their noise

which made the snow, the swarm, more silent. More welcome.
I could have watched for hours and seen nothing more than specks

against the light interrupting light and away from it, flying blind
but carrying light, specks becoming atoms. They flew too fast

to become snow itself, flying in a random panic, looming close
but disappearing, like flakes on the tongue, at the point of recognition.

They died as they landed, riding on their own melting as poems do
and in the morning there was nothing to be seen of them.

Instead, a streak of lemon, lemon honey, ringed the sky
but the cloud-lid never lifted, the weekend promised a blizzard.

I could have watched for hours and seen nothing more than I do now,
an image, metaphor, but not the blind imperative that drove them.

John Kinsella

REVERSE ANTHROPOMORPHISM

These birds – western flyeaters – are sizing
me up, making me within their own image,
moi-même, at least for the purpose of hunting.
Through glass, I watch them target their prey,
insects in the temporal zone of the verandah:

one flyeater darts out to seize an insect flyer,
then returns to watch his companion do the same.
The whole time they both keep an eye on me. *Moi-même.*
I connect with them in no way. No displacement
to fill the page: no female pushing a pram

full of letters, 'protecting the male'. Empirically,
they are male *and* female. It seems they perform
the *same* tactics, the same roles when hunting. Role-play?
Who am I to say? Some *would* say it's a matter
of knowing what to look for. *Moi-même.*

This is not a rare experience, it happens most days.
We have grown familiar. Don't mistake my indifference
for their indifference, or their relaxation
for a reflection of mine. We do not share.
Though I am touched that they are near.

And they manage to get done what they
need to get done. It's rich pickings
near where I sit, separated by the glass window,
insects making their own conversations,
losing lives. *Moi-même.* Role-play.

James Lasdun

I'm trying to solve the problem of the paths
between the beds. A six-inch cover
of cedar chips that took a month to lay
rotted in two years and turned to weeds.
I scraped them up and carted them away,
then planted half a sack of clover seeds
for a 'living mulch'. I liked that: flowers
strewn along like stars, the cupid's bow
drawn on each leaf like thumbnail quartermoons,
its easy, springy give – until it spread
under the split trunks framing off each bed,
scribbling them over in its own
green graffiti... I ripped it out
and now I'm trying to set these paths in stone.
It isn't hard to find: the ground here's littered
with rough-cut slabs, some of them so vast
you'd think a race of giants must have lived here
building some bluestone Carnac or Stonehenge,
us their dwindled offspring, foraging
among their ruins... I scavenge
lesser pieces; pry them from the clutches
of tree-roots, lift them out of ditches,
filch them from our own stone wall
guiltily, though they're mine to take,
then wrestle them on board the two-wheeled dolly
and drag them up the driveway to the fence,
where, in a precarious waltz, I tip
and twist them backward, tilting all their weight
first on one corner, then the other
and dance them slowly through the garden gate.
The hard part's next, piecing them together;
a matter of blind luck and infinite pains:
one eye open for the god-given fit –

this stone's jagged key to that one's lock –
the other quietly gauging how to fudge it:
split the difference on angles, cram the gaps
with stone-dust filler; hoping what the rains
don't wash away, the frost will pack and harden...
A chipmunk blinks and watches from his rock,
wondering if I've lost my mind perhaps.
Perhaps I have; out here every day,
cultivating – no, not even that;
tending the inverse spaces of my garden
(it's like a blueprint now, for Bluebeard's castle),
while outside, by degrees, the planet slips
– a locking piece – into apocalypse,
but somehow I can't tear myself away:
I like the drudgery; I seem to revel
in pitting myself against the sheer
recalcitrance of the stones; using
their awkwardness – each cupped or bulging face,
every cockeyed bevel and crooked curve,
each quirk of outline (this one a cracked lyre,
that one more like a severed head) –
to send a flickering pulse along the border
so that it seems to ripple round each bed
with an unstonelike, liquid grace:
'the best stones in the best possible order'
or some such half-remembered rule in mind,
as if it mattered, making some old stones
say or be anything but stone, stone, stone;
as if these paths might serve some purpose
aside from making nothing happen; as if
their lapidary line might lead me somewhere –
inward, onward, upward, anywhere
other than merely back where I began,
wondering where I've been, and what I've done.

Glyn Maxwell

Hard to remember, now there is nothing here,
that there was once nothing here. Hard to remember
they paused in a field with a plot for a field and a feel
of a place in mind and a little knot of horses
      faraway in a corner stood there

pretty much where that little knot of horses
stands. The railway ran through the white template,
the life and death of it, made east and west
of nowhere. North and south it left itself
      whichever way one looked.

Hard to remember now that it's all begun
that it all began and, now that it's all over,
hard to recall it's gone. Those who are gone
arrive in a crest of steam and the late-lamented
      help them with their boxes.

Those to the east have a shed and those to the west
a greenhouse, it was a field and not a field
hereafter, it was a path through new houses
and a sweetshop. There was a lane and another lane
      which, crossing it, was obliged

to name it what it was named and the five things
needed they built buildings for. A meadow
reared its set of gardens like farm-children
edging behind houses to belong there,
      to cluster and imagine

a gate that is always shut will be always open.
But for now the horizon was sky and a blackberry hedge
and the north was the nettle-bed, and the south the roses
and the east an archway to those sad allotments,
       and the west a banded twilight

as out they build, in the time a bedtime story
takes to ferry me shipshape to tomorrow;
out they build till I wake and the horizon's
gone. It won't be found until it's wept to
       on a holiday. The town

is mine, this side of town is mine, the homes
go strolling by, then, bowing out of sight
they scurry round the world to be back in time
for when I pass, as if they never budged,
       and a chuckle of wood-chimes

is all I'll ever know. Now they grow names
with care, they name what dreams of being garden
Garden, what will never be a city
City, and they name it for some hovels
       in the Domesday Book. Go where

they say it is. Come to where I'm from.
The north is lost in thought: the glance away
from fairy tales is a look through time, the south
is sitting me down and standing me up, the east
       unnerves me with its look:

I never heard of west, what's west? and the west
goes west in search of answers. Hard to remember
I know what I mean, now nothing's left but a lawn
and me knowing what I mean. The place spread out
       like anything being thought of

reddens in shame and joy. So I was thought of,
for the north was a copse of houses to be called at,
found wanting at, found wanting *you*, while the south
got London like one gets a belief and beamed
      to find it all leads somewhere.

The east I met in dreams was the east I knew
but enormous, so the west escorted me
where those like me *liked* me, on a singing bus-ride
I prayed would never end till I begged it to.
      Things come true, looking back,

things come true I was wishing for, they are gone
and still come true, when north south east and west
flop on a lawn in summer and so do you,
and the time I stare at you and you do
      are the same time, are equal,

the same time, same span, like an equals sign
is suddenly loop-the-looping home so it forms
infinity by a hedge in summer – *You*,
I caught your eye in my life. What else did I do?
      and the longer ago it gets

the longer it lasts and closer it seems to come.
Come to where I'll never again be from,
you, there are miracles showing up again
instead of us. The shadows comb the lawn,
      diligent and discreet

as a search team until I call it off
for want of a clue. South go the memories,
north goes love as I wake, while the east and west
welcome the bright apprentice and dispatch him
      daily on his amiable

fruitless errand. My eyes grow books and suffer
books, my ears grow songs and suffer songs,
my hands break news, my feet fetch drinks, my stomach
stomachs it all like something bet it it couldn't,
        and out they build, they build,

from the soft incessant fountain they began with,
to the homes we knew and will never, side by side
they build them, like the ones we won't remember
play tag in the park with the ones we can't forget
        and the kids they brought together

had kids together and soon the north was the poems
I wrote about you, woods of poems I pass through
guided by a voice in headphones, soon
the south is the realm of Alfie Rose, the east
        an airport serving nowhere

and the west the news I brush off like a boy-king
as I stir the foam and find I'm in Manhattan.
And maybe they built out far enough, I wonder,
sipping the wine in a brasserie I always
        loved, or I text my exes

in the terminal or I listen to the songs
I listen to. At the rendezvous of evening
I always miss for mulling over headlines,
what travelled outward travels at standstill,
        then starts to travel in,

when the woodland path arrives in the blue clearing:
the youngest lad of three is getting ready
to set some last adventure with his soldiers.
But his pals who don't take no for an answer shriek
        from the road until he rises,

childhood done forever. The clearing reached,
the path is weeds and litter. Hard to remember,
now I've everything, that I once had everything,
and I drive through a north I cried in, where the council's
  nailed up signs and arrows

that *These are trees* and *So are these*, and the south
is so far south it's south of understanding,
and the east is the internet and the west my time here
googled with a whisky. Come to where
  I said it was, it's there

I'm gone. The plastic infantryman
dropped in the wood outlasts the wood. I meet you
for the last time but one on a rainy Thursday,
and the street rolls up behind me like a script
  unless I turn to stop it.

The fine idea remains just that. The blueprint
flutters down unused, and the children's children
tweet on the ragged swings. There's not a tree,
a yard of light, a lamp-post that won't
  tap from me my only

soliloquy *I remember when we,
when she*, declining, like an old-school verb,
to *when you*. Then you, derailed at a dream-junction,
are someone else again, the old first names
  step out in their parish beauty,

Rosemary, Clare, Diane… What I want from one
is what I got from one, as if the maths
made sense in the negative: now writing looks
like black on white but feels like flint on nothing.
  North they are shutting up

the picture book forever, south the theatre's
pricey card for children, east the warehouse
eats the one beside it, west I set out
seats for relatives and replay scenes
        that happened in the west,

right there I mutter, peering into sunset,
pulling a cork among abandoned deck-chairs.
Come to where I'm from, like the bloke I once
got talking to in The Sun, on the only night
        he spent in my birthplace,

a desolate Sunday evening wiping tables
and he said *I hate it here* and he was gone,
said he'd never come again, come again like him,
when you never will, come to where I'm from
        like the glossy editor

in Soho who confided in me *Glyn,*
it does you no favours, saying where you're from:
say you're 'from Hertfordshire', come again like him,
where you wouldn't be seen dead. Come again like one
        who's lost, come again like one

for seconds on First Capital Connect,
who meant to lift his eyelids from his iPhone
as the little place shot by but when he looks
we're on Brunel's old viaduct, gone, bygone,
        high over the green fields

and lanes of where I'm from. The north is a new
flowerbed from who knows when, the south
four 4x4s on a driveway, in the east
a fellow stops to stare at where we lived
        as if he remembered us

when he lived, I remember him well enough, and the west
is me at work on this by the garden gate.
Preposterous, what was. I watch that gate
for you and all the gone. The odds against
	are stars to sail between.

Come to where I'm from. Now there's nothing here,
hard to remember once there was nothing here.
Hard to remember we paused in a field in sunshine
with a plot for a field and a feel of a place in mind
	and a little knot of horses

faraway in a corner stood right there
near where those horses stand, by the quiet trees,
beyond which all the yellow rising hills
you think are there are the yellow rising hills
	you thought were there.

Richard Meier

In what for you was something of a departure,
you bought me this lovely, if demanding, gift
for Christmas. After lunch I held it aloft
by various trees and fence-posts till we thought

we'd found its ideal spot, so we could watch.
Or I could, since you'd left me by the time,
an untouched fortnight later, I first noticed
the seed level had dropped. Bit by bit

it would fall daily and, since one tense wren
was all I'd glimpsed come near the thing, I saw
how lightly there you'd always been; and how
it could sustain me, your being here alone.

Esther Morgan

GRACE

You've been living for this for weeks
without knowing it:

the moment the house empties like a city in August
so completely
it forgets you exist.

Light withdraws slowly
is almost gone before you notice.

In the stillness, everything becomes itself:
the circle of white plates on the kitchen table
the serious chairs that attend them

even the roses on the papered walls
seem to open a little wider.

It looks simple: the glass vase holding
whatever is offered –
cut flowers, or the thought of them –

simple, though not easy
this waiting without hunger in the near dark
for what you may be about to receive.

Sandeep Parmar

Her Face, Which Does Not Lie

Porcelain is the colour of her skin.
It is also other things entirely.
How to reconcile this fact? It is impossible
to forget that she too was other things.
Who was this vessel
and what made him drink?
Was it the spirit of that river
it is a wonder anyone can remember?
Its name must have been written
by one who, like a jealous wife,
covets the photograph of her husband's mistress.

In German, the word *Porzellan*
does not sound like something
that could be easily broken.
Nor does it seem fitting that such a thing
should lay between two people
who sit together in silence at a table
considering its many other meanings.

'Names are memories of things',
the wife reminds him.
But he remembers differently and so
every now and again when she is alone
she holds the photograph up to the light
to test the quality of her suspicions.

Tom Paulin

A NOTICED THING

The windsock by the airfield
it's hanging flaccid this evening
– hanging flaccid on its white pole
by the perimeter
I happen on it this hot humid Friday
like the way you find *a symbol*
in a poem or a novel
– something that's over- or predetermined
– something like that
or like this too obvious giant condom
with the teat snipped off
which takes us back to the static
empty windsock drained of its usual orange colour
– your name is on me it says
on me like a bullet
I can tell you're shocked
well just a tad you are
at being spoken to by a flat
– you called me flaccid –
by a flat windsock
– let me remind you
I was your image at one time
for the whole world
for everything-that-is-the-case
plus the wind rushing through it
or gulshing through it if you like
but perhaps you've moved on?
As you can see I'm all used up
like some friend you've left behind
– the world though is not conclusion
stuff that in your sock and ate it

Leeanne Quinn

THE IMPACT

It is late evening when the shouts
of local boys and girls begin. Across this city
street they shoot footballs, bottle tops,
hot chips from the chip shop whose steadfast
neon light shines opposite my window,
more dependable than summer sun.
Car horns bleat intermittently, or tyres break
to a dead halt, and each time I look out
I expect to see some body flung
far from itself, broken to a new form –
but the cars only ever move on, trailing
coarse words that elicit appreciative roars.
As evening darkens and turns the windows
of vacant houses black, they gather under
the light of a lamppost, blow cigarette smoke
in fat rings that grow thin, imperfect halos.
As the smoke reaches a bouquet of flowers
tied above them on the lamppost,
I wonder if they know what misfortune
it marks – though wilting now, I often wake
to see them blooming. As they begin
to move on, a small boy flicks
the butt of his cigarette at the windscreen
of an oncoming car, his parting gesture.
For a moment the embers flare
magnificently, a cheer goes up
in recognition of the boy, his daring,
the unexpected beauty of the impact.

Peter Robinson

LIKE A FOREIGN COUNTRY

That much would have to be explained:
how cloud-roofs at dawn
were burned off by a July sun
and showers washed out washing day,
how identity theft protection
or laundry would get done
when there was the tax disc to display.

It was time, time to cultivate our garden
where blades of whitened grass
hid creatures still alive
beneath their mossy stone,
or in a creosoted shed
with ivy bursting through its boards –
still lives of paint cans, and so on.

That much had been left behind.
Cloud-diffused sunlight would soothe
my jangled nerves. You'd find
it was like our daughter's school report:
me too, I'm happy as can be
expected, coping well
with moving… in a foreign country.

Days gone, terraces, terra incognita,
were like our faces redefined
at a bathroom mirror when it's cleaned;
for time had taken its advantage
over us, the gained
and lost perspectives realigned.
That much would have to be explained.

Kathryn Simmonds

WHEN SIX O'CLOCK COMES AND ANOTHER DAY HAS PASSED

the baby who can not speak, speaks to me.
When the sun has risen and set over the same dishes
and the predicted weather is white cloud,
the baby steadies her head which is the head of a drunk's
and holds me with her filmic blue eyes
and all at once we stop half-heartedly row, rowing
our boat and see each other clear
in the television's orange glow. She regards me,
the baby who does not know a television from a table lamp,
the baby, who is so heavy with other people's hopes
she has no body to call her own,
the baby who is forever being shifted, rearranged,
whose hands must be unfurled and wiped with cotton wool
whose scalp must be combed of cradle cap,
the baby who has exactly no memories
softens her face in the early evening light and says I understand.

Jon Stone

Near Extremes 1

Where I come from, it's the other way round:
we plunk cinder knucklebones into our soda,
stand hunched over momentary snowflakes,
willing our fags to catch cold, so we can
scorch our lips with frost-feathered plumes.

It gets chilly. It gets close.
As errants, we'd slosh turps on a Guy,
poke with a match and go bubble-cheeked
with urchin glee as he fleshed out in snow.
We never seemed to earn that white hot Christmas.

Adam Thorpe

Sutton Hoo

The Overflow Car Park's empty,
the light a lustrous grey on birch.

The local farmer's cut his turf
right to the ligeance, so it's just this corner,

discreetly fenced in wire. A spellbound
darkness of firs at the field's edge.

Several shaggy swells: which one?
With history's mood-swings it's hard

to tell. There's gold for some, though;
while my sense of nation's less a buried crown

than a stain of post-hole, or this viewing
rostrum I try to work things out from.

David Troupes

The Simple Man Arriving Through the Fields

Throw myself down and here's my camp –
under the thorn,
in the rolls
of gruff weed, in the fingers

of a new warmth. Stars
pop in the black and slowly
I align myself
like the needle and cork floated for a compass

Mother! Such an endlessness –
the byways and nighways
which are all I need of home.
Tomorrow morning,

early, when the sun is a tray of crumbs
I'll rise
in the spin and wander,
till I throw myself down and there's my urn.

Samantha Wynne-Rhydderch

In the end we turned him into a verb:
to pont meaning *to pose in ice and snow*

until frozen. On the voyage south he'd be
tilting plates in the darkroom, in one hand

the developing dish, in the other a basin
of vomit. One minute he'd arrange us

in groups for the cinematograph, then rush
to the ship's side. Once Ponco roped up

his JA Prestwich over *Terra Nova's* bow,
balanced on three planks. He lost the tip

of his tongue when it stuck to the camera
at thirty below. Corneas can freeze

to peep-sight. At one hundred degrees
of frost the film's ribbon will split.

To pont would also mean *pontificate*. He'd insist
on reeling the film slowly to prevent

sparks. We'd rehearse the Pole Picture:
mount the camera on the theodolite tripod,

wind twine over the trigger and guide it
round a ski stick to get the direction right.

He'd instruct us on setting the shutter, how to
use a flash in the tent with quarter of an inch of powder

and F11. En route to the Pole I sent back
negatives with the support teams, a sheet

torn from my sledging log detailing exposure
data; how composed we were, how cold.

Jane Yeh

Yesterday,

The black cat that always sits on the bin next door wasn't sitting on
the bin.
- The price of porcine commodities rose slightly, while that of the
vegetarian English breakfast at my local café remained
the same.
- No-one attempted to assassinate the French librarian at my old
university, despite his insistence on labelling paperback
books 'INFÉRIEUR'.
- The last of the flannelette pyjama tops I had stocked up on in
America abruptly gave up the ghost.

Something was missing from my life (other than the black cat and
pyjama tops).
- A new recycling regimen in my borough wasn't enough to make
up for it.
- Neither were reports of recent advances in tooth-whitening,
fuel injection, and women's rights in various countries.
- Nor did a certain Hollywood actor's growing resemblance to
Mayor McCheese prove sufficiently distracting.

The shallowness of my existence was hardly a novel development.
- I had been known to frequent discount shopping outlets voluntarily
and to reject suitors based solely on hair length.
- I spent hours devising ingenious interrogation tactics for Cluedo,
despite having no-one to play with.
- I was a card-carrying member of a secret organisation devoted to
the abolition of Velcro.

It was unclear to me whether literature could offer any salvation.
- Volatility in German type markets meant that italics were now
verboten.
- The invention of see-through paper resulted in a move towards
blatant transparency in fiction.

- A sort of massive rise in textual ambiguity rendered the love poem obsolete… or did it?

Eventually I grew weary of thinking on these conundrums.
- The neighbour's hideous spaniel popped out for a moment and gave me a soulful look.
- The number of charitable donations to Battersea Dogs' Home I planned to make one day subsequently decreased to zero.
- Scientists declared there was a 60% chance that hell would freeze over due to climate change, while Streatham would remain unaffected.
- A level 5 pollen alert led to extreme hoovering, even inside my hermetically sealed castle.

Publisher acknowledgements

Emily Berry · LETTER TO HUSBAND · Times Literary Supplement

Ruth Bidgood · JOY · *Above the Forests* · Cinnamon Press

Beverley Bie Brahic · WHITE SHEETS · ON THE PATHETIC FALLACY ·
White Sheets · CB Editions

Kate Bingham · OPEN · Times Literary Supplement

Sean Borodale · 10TH FEBRUARY: QUEEN · *Bee Journal* · Jonathan Cape

Dan Burt · SLOWLY SOUNDS THE BELL · *We Look Like This* · Carcanet Press

Jennifer Clarvoe · THAT WAY · *Counter-Amores* · University of Chicago Press

John Clegg · MERMAIDS · *Antler* · Salt Publishing

Anne Cluysenaar · MOON · *Migrations* · Cinnamon Press

Loretta Collins Klobah · LA MADONNA URBANA · PECKHAM, LONDON, COLD
WATER FLAT · *The Twelve-Foot Neon Woman* · Peepal Tree Press

Julia Copus · THIS IS THE POEM IN WHICH I HAVE NOT LEFT YOU ·
The World's Two Smallest Humans · Faber and Faber

Carol Ann Duffy · WATER · *The Bees* · Picador

Helen Dunmore · THE MALARKEY · *The Malarkey* · Bloodaxe Books

Paul Durcan · SUNNY HILL · *Praise in Which I Live and Move and Have
My Being* · Harvill Secker

Rhian Edwards · SKYPE · GIRL MEATS BOY · *Clueless Dogs* · Seren

Helen Farish · A NIGHT IN AT NOHANT · *Nocturnes at Nohant* · Bloodaxe Books

Paul Farley · THE POWER · *The Dark Film* · Picador

James Fenton · AT THE KERB · *Yellow Tulips* · Faber and Faber

Jorie Graham · CAGNES SUR MER · THE BIRD ON MY RAILING · *Place* ·
Carcanet Press

Philip Gross · NOT SAYING · *Deep Field* · Bloodaxe

Marilyn Hacker · *Fugue on a Line of Amr bin M'ad Yakrib* ·
The Wolf Magazine

Lucy Hamilton · LANDMARKS & BOUNDARIES · THE CHAIR · *Stalker* ·
Shearsman Books

Geoff Hattersley · NO ONE KNOWS WHY · The North

Oli Hazzard · FOUR LANDSCAPES · *Between Two Windows* · Carcanet Press

David Herd · 3 NOTES TOWARDS A LOVE SONG · *All Just* · Carcanet Press

Barry Hill · BOY WITH A PIGEON, 1944 · NARCISSUS, 1950 · *Naked Clay:
Drawing from Lucian Freud* · Shearsman Books

Geoffrey Hill · IV · XXVIII · *Odi Barbare* · Clutag Press

Selima Hill · Muriel · The Elephant is Much Too Big to Boogie · *People Who Like Meatballs* · Bloodaxe Books

Jane Hirshfield · The Supple Deer · *Come, Thief* · Bloodaxe Books

Julith Jedamus · Barn Burning, Fall River, Wisconsin, July 1966 · *The Swerve* · Carcanet Press

Mimi Khalvati · The Swarm · Poetry Review

John Kinsella · Mea Culpa: Cleaning the Gutters · The Warwick Review

John Kinsella · Reverse Anthropomorphism · *Armour* · Picador

James Lasdun · Stones · *Water Sessions* · Jonathan Cape

Michael Longley · Marigolds, 1960 · London Review of Books

Glyn Maxwell · Come to Where I'm From · Poetry Review

Richard Meier · The Feeder · *Misadventure* · Picador

Esther Morgan · Grace · *Grace* · Bloodaxe Books

Sandeep Parmar · Her Face, Which Does Not Lie · *The Marble Orchard* · Shearsman Books

Tom Paulin · A Noticed Thing · *Love's Bonfire* · Faber and Faber

Leeanne Quinn · The Impact · *Before You* · Dedalus Press

Denise Riley · A Part Song · London Review of Books

Sam Riviere · Fall in Love All Over Again · Buffering 15% · *81 Austerities* · Faber and Faber

Peter Robinson · Like a Foreign Country · *The Returning Sky* · Shearsman Books

Jacob Sam-La Rose · After Lazerdrome, McDonalds, Peckham Rye · How to be Gravity · *Breaking Silence* · Bloodaxe Books

Kathryn Simmonds · When Six O'Clock Comes and Another Day Has Passed · The North

Greta Stoddart · Deep Sea Diver · Magma Poetry

Jon Stone · Near Extremes i · *School of Forgery* · Salt

Adam Thorpe · Sutton Hoo · *Voluntary* · Jonathan Cape

David Troupes · The Simple Man Arriving Through the Fields · *The Simple Men* · Two Ravens Press

Samantha Wynne-Rhydderch · Ponting · *Banjo* · Picador

Jane Yeh · Yesterday, · PN Review 202